Light Fantastic

Library Edition Published 1990

Published by Marshall Cavendish Corporation
147 West Merrick Road
Freeport, Long Island
N.Y. 11520

Printed in Italy by New Interlitho, Milan

© Marshall Cavendish Limited 1989
© Cherrytree Press Limited 1988

Library Edition produced by DPM Services Limited

Library of Congress Cataloging-in-Publication Data

Kerrod, Robin.
    Light fantastic / by Robin Kerrod: illustrated by Mike Atkinson and Sarah Atkinson.
        p. cm. – (Secrets of science : 5)
    "A Cherrytree book."
    Includes index
    Summary: A collection of science activities demonstrating the properties of light.
        1. Light – Experiments – Juvenile literature.[1. Light – Experiments
    2. Experiments.]
        I. Atkinson, Mike. [1]. II. Atkinson, Sarah, [1]. III. Title.
        IV. Series: Kerrod, Robin, Secrets of science : 5.
    QC385.K47 1989
    635'.078 – dc20   89-998
                                                                  CIP
                                                                  AC

ISBN 1-85435-156-7
ISBN 1-85435-151-6(set)

SECRETS OF SCIENCE

Light Fantastic

Robin Kerrod

Illustrated by Mike Atkinson
and Sarah Atkinson

MARSHALL CAVENDISH
NEW YORK · LONDON · TORONTO · SYDNEY

Safety First

☐ Ask an adult for permission before you start any experiment, especially if you are using matches or anything hot, sharp, or poisonous.

☐ Don't wear good clothes. Wear old ones or an apron.

☐ If you work on a table, use an old one and protect it with paper or cardboard.

☐ Do water experiments in the sink, on the draining board, or outdoors.

☐ Strike matches away from your body, and make sure they are out before you throw them away.

☐ Make sure candles are standing securely.

☐ Wear oven gloves when handling anything hot.

☐ Be careful when cutting things. Always cut away from your body.

☐ Don't use tin cans with jagged edges. Use those with lids.

☐ Use only safe children's glue, glue sticks, or paste.

☐ **Never** taste chemicals, unless the book tells you to.

☐ Label all bottles and jars containing chemicals, and store them where young children can't get at them – and never in the family's food cupboard.

☐ Never use or play with electricity. It can KILL. Use a battery to create a current if needed.

☐ When you have finished an experiment, put your things away, clean up, and wash your hands.

Contents

Light in the Darkness

The sun is a fiery star millions and millions of miles away in space. Even though it is so far away, the sun glows brightly enough to light our planet, earth.

During the day, you can see the sun as it travels across the sky. In the evening, the sun goes down, and night falls. When it is dark, we have to switch on the electric light to see by.

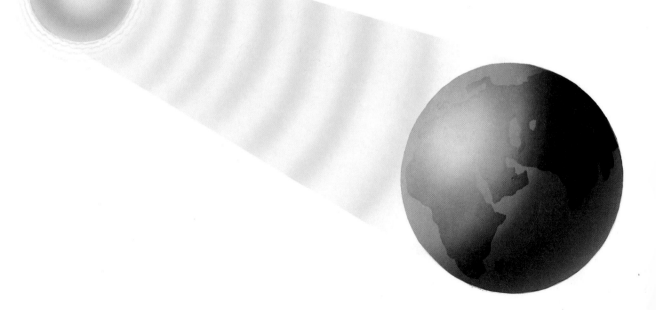

Lightning Strike
Electricity in the air causes lightning. It makes light when it jumps between the clouds.

Firefly Glow
Some beetles, called fireflies, glow in the dark. Chemicals in their bodies make light.

Flick a Switch
When you switch on a light, electricity heats up the wire in the light bulb and makes it glow.

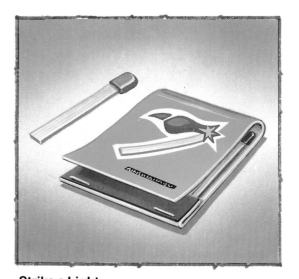

Strike a Light
When you strike a match, the head bursts into flame. It sets fire to the stick and makes light.

Shadows and Sundials

A shadow is a dark patch on the ground which the sunlight cannot reach because your body, or some other object, is in the way.

Have you noticed how shadows move around during the day? They move with the sun. One day, mark the position on the ground of the shadow of a tree at, say, 11 o'clock. Next day, note the time when the shadow falls in the same place. Yes, it will be 11 o'clock.

The sun is always in the same place at the same time, and so are the shadows it makes. You can use shadows to make a shadow clock – like this old-fashioned sundial.

Make a Sundial

1 You need a stick about 8 inches long; a large plant pot; a piece of cardboard; a clock or watch – for one day.

2 Cut a cardboard circle the same size as the top of the pot, and make a hole in the middle.

3 Push the stick through the cardboard and through the upturned pot, so the stick stands upright.

4 Place the pot in the sun early in the morning. Mark where the shadow of the stick falls on every hour. Next day, you can use your sundial to tell the time.

Shadow Play

You can use shadows to make pictures on the wall. All you need are your hands, a dark room, and a flashlight or lamp.

First, switch off all the lights except for your flashlight or lamp. Then, hold your hands close to the wall so that their shadow is sharp. Place your fingers and thumbs in different positions to make shadows that look like the heads of animals or people.

Guess which animals these are supposed to be. Can you make them?

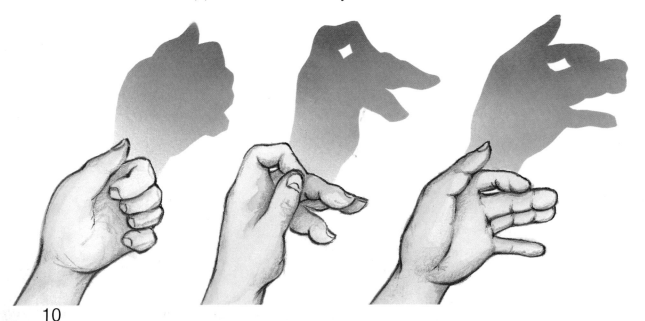

Give a shadow puppet show. To make the puppets, draw the outline of figures on stiff cardboard and then cut them out. Tape the figures to the ends of thin sticks. You could also make wire figures.

Hang up an old sheet as a screen. Behind the screen, hold up your puppets in the light from a flashlight or lamp. The shadows will fall on the screen and be seen by your audience in front. Be sure to make up a good story for the puppets to act.

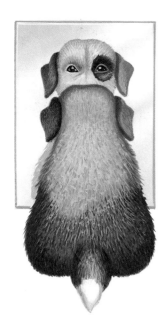

Mirror, Mirror on the Wall

If you look at a piece of glass, you see through it. If you look at a mirror, you see yourself. Mirrors reflect, or send back, light that falls on them. They are made of glass, with a silvery coating on the back. It is this shiny coating that reflects the light.

When you look in a mirror, you do not see yourself as others see you. You are the wrong way around, like this sum.

When Patch the dog looks in the mirror, he sees his black eye on the right. We see it on the left. The picture in the mirror is called a mirror image. In a mirror image, everything is changed from left to right.

To see himself as we see him, Patch needs another mirror. If he looks in this second mirror set at a right angle to the first one, he will see himself as he really is. The second mirror forms a mirror image of the mirror image in the first mirror. Try it for yourself!

Patterns of Light

You can make beautiful patterns with mirrors. Stand two mirrors at an angle to each other with their edges touching. Place some objects in between and look down at them in the mirrors. See how they form a circle of images.

The objects are reflected in the mirrors several times. This is the idea behind the kaleidoscope, one of the most amazing toys ever invented.

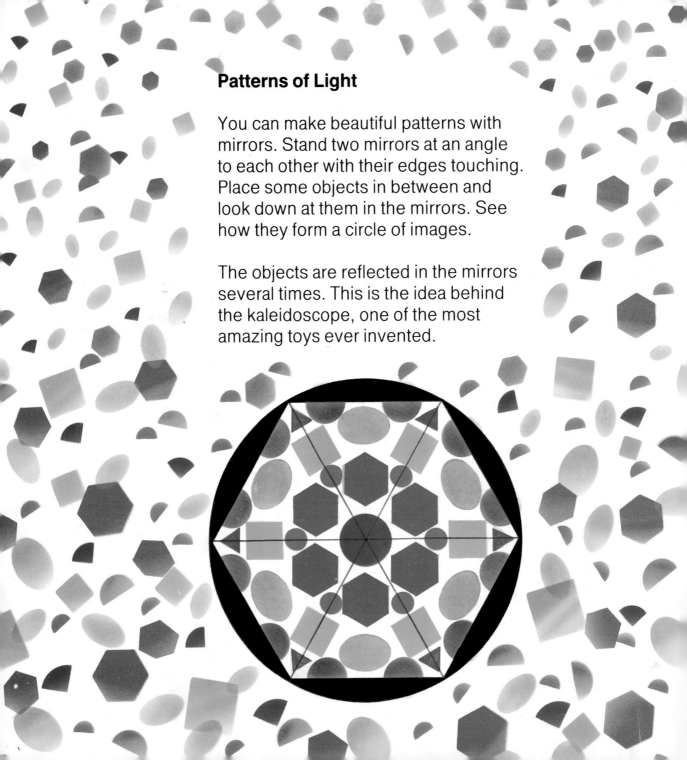

Make a Kaleidoscope

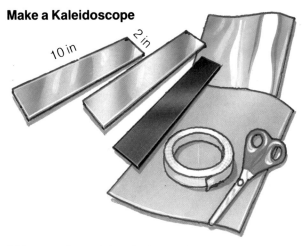

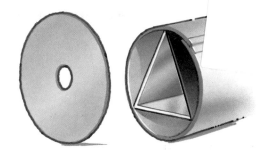

1 You need an adult to help; two long narrow mirrors the same size; a piece of stiff black cardboard the same size; cardboard; bits of colored paper; plastic film; tape.

2 Tape the mirrors together along one edge. Between them, tape the black cardboard to make a triangular tube.

3 Roll a sheet of cardboard around the triangle to make a tube, and tape it firmly.

4 Cut out a circle of cardboard to fit over one end of the tube, and tape it in position. Make a small hole in the middle to look through.

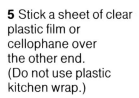

5 Stick a sheet of clear plastic film or cellophane over the other end. (Do not use plastic kitchen wrap.)

6 Then sprinkle on tiny pieces of colored paper. Cover them with another sheet of clear film.

Your kaleidoscope is now ready. Hold it up to the light, and look at the lovely patterns it makes. See how they change if you tap the tube to shift the pieces of paper.

Around the Corner, Over the Wall

Light travels in straight lines, so you cannot see around corners – unless you have a mirror. If you hold your mirror just around the corner at an angle, you will be able to see what is happening. You can do the same thing to look over a wall.

In both cases, what you see will be a mirror image, not a true picture. You need two mirrors to see a true picture.

To look over the wall, hold one mirror high above your head and facing over the wall. Hold the other below it facing you. Tilt the mirrors until you can see over the wall. Light is being reflected from the top one to the bottom one.

You can make an instrument that uses mirrors in this way, called a periscope.

Make a Periscope

1 You need an adult to help; a large sheet of stiff cardboard; two small flat mirrors; tape; a ruler; a protractor.

2 Divide the sheet of cardboard into four equal strips, and score it so that it will bend.

3 Cut out windows, and make slots the width of the mirrors. Use the protractor to make sure they are at an angle of 45°.

4 Fold the cardboard to form a square tube, and tape the edges together. Tape pieces of cardboard over the ends.

5 Slide the mirrors into the slots so that they face out through the windows.

Your periscope is now ready for use. What is over the wall?

Funny Face

When you look in an ordinary, flat mirror, your image is the same size and shape as you are. But there are some mirrors that are curved, and they change the way you look.

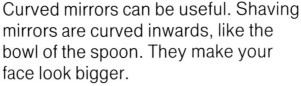

You can see how curved mirrors change things by looking in a shiny spoon. Look at your face in both sides of the spoon. How does it change?

Curved mirrors can be useful. Shaving mirrors are curved inwards, like the bowl of the spoon. They make your face look bigger.

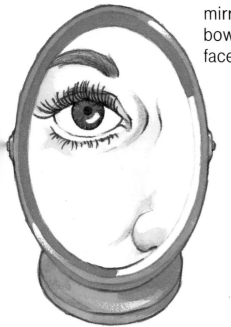

18

Side mirrors on cars are curved the other way. They make things look smaller, but let the driver see over a wider area.

You can also have fun with curved mirrors. At some amusement parks, there are special mirrors curved to make you look silly. You can appear to have the neck of a giraffe, the body of a hippopotamus, and the legs of a dachshund!

Bending Light

Put a straw in a glass of water, and see what happens to it. It looks bent or even chopped in two at some angles.

The bend or break takes place at the surface of the water. It happens because light bends when it passes from one substance to another.

We call the bending of light **refraction**. We call substances that allow light to pass through **transparent**. Water, air, and glass are transparent.

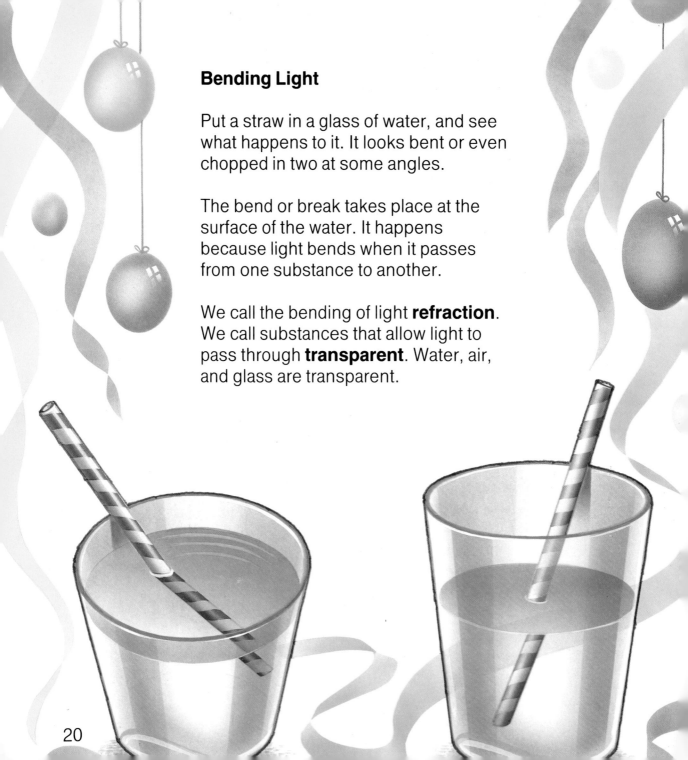

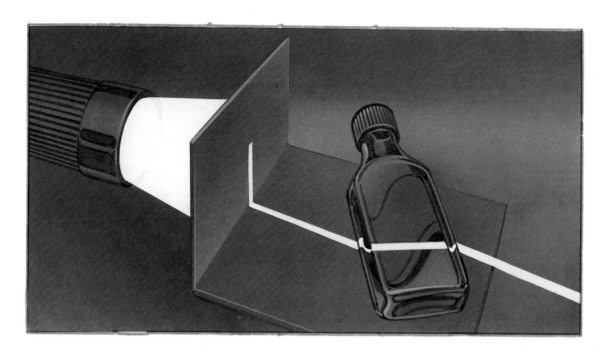

See how light bends in this simple
experiment. You need a flashlight,
some cardboard, and a bottle with a
tight-fitting cap full of water. Bend the
cardboard in an L-shape and cut a slit in
the upright part. In a dark room, shine
the flashlight through the slit so that a
narrow beam comes out. Put the bottle
in the way, and see how it changes the
direction of the light beam.

Notice that the light is bent twice – once
when it goes into the bottle, and once
when it comes out.

One in the Eye

Hold one side of a glass of water (make sure it is dry) against this page and look through the other side. See how the letters are magnified, or made bigger.

The glass is acting as a lens. A lens is anything transparent that bends light because of its shape. A magnifying glass curves outward. It is thick in the middle and thin at the edge.

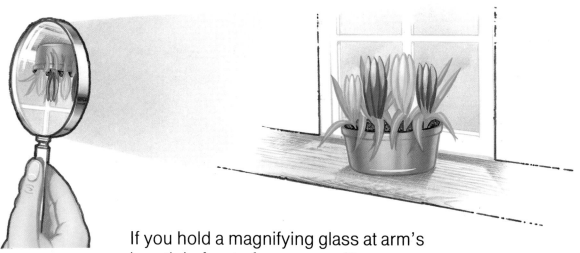

If you hold a magnifying glass at arm's length in front of you, you will see a smaller image of whatever is in front of you – but upside down. If you hold a piece of paper just behind the glass, you will see the image on the paper.

The lens in your eye works in the same way. It forms a sharp image at the back of your eye. It focuses the image. The lens in a camera does the same.

Seeing Near and Far

Try to get hold of two magnifying glasses. Hold one in your left hand at arm's length, and you will see in it a small, upside-down picture. Hold the other glass in your left hand close to your eye, and move the glass in your right hand toward you until you can see a sharp image. The image is now larger, though it is still upside down.

What you have done is to show how a telescope works. A telescope makes things appear bigger and closer.

Astronomers, scientists who study the stars, use telescopes because the stars are so far away. You can make a telescope yourself. It won't see into outer space, but it will be fun to use.

You will need two lenses. Magnifying glasses will do, but it is far better to buy a cheap pair of real lenses. Ask for one lens with a long focal length, say 20 inches; and the other with a short focal length, say one inch.

Make a Telescope

1 You need two lenses (see text); two sheets of cardboard, which are black on one side; glue.

2 Hold up your lenses as you did before to see roughly how far apart they should be to give the best magnification. This will also tell you how long to make your telescope.

3 Roll up the cardboard into two tubes that fit around the lenses, and fit one inside the other. Make sure the black side is inside to stop light from being reflected.

4 Put the lenses in the tubes, gluing them in place with rings cut from the tubes. Glue each tube firmly.

5 Put one tube inside the other, and your telescope is ready. Slide the inner tube in and out to focus, or make the image sharp.

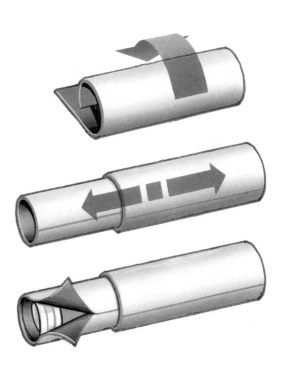

Over the Rainbow

Have you ever looked at all the colors in a bubble – the colors of the rainbow. Blow some bubbles, and see what you can see in them. Look for violet, indigo, blue, green, yellow, orange, red. (Indigo is dark blue).

Where do the colors come from? They come from sunlight. Sunlight is made up of light of many colors, which mix together to make white. Make a color wheel to see how the colors mix.

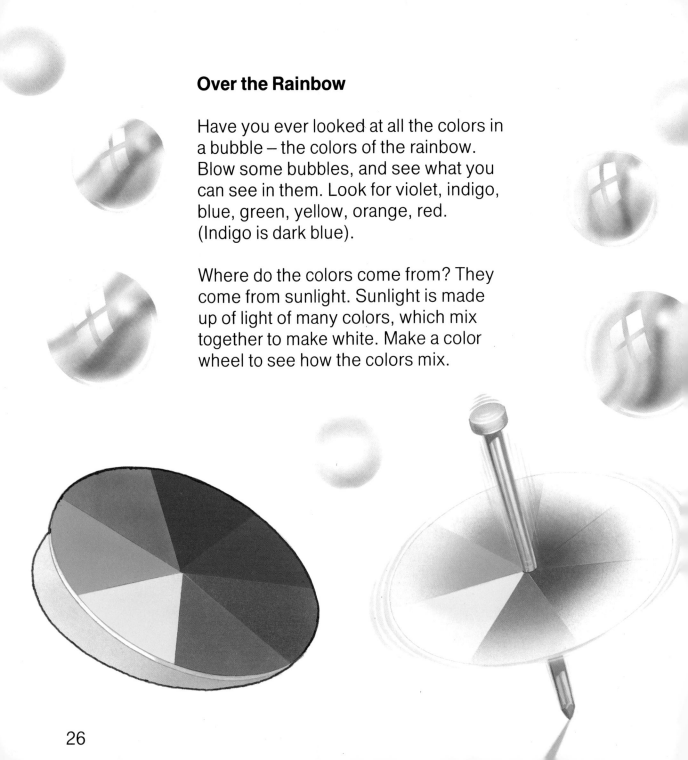

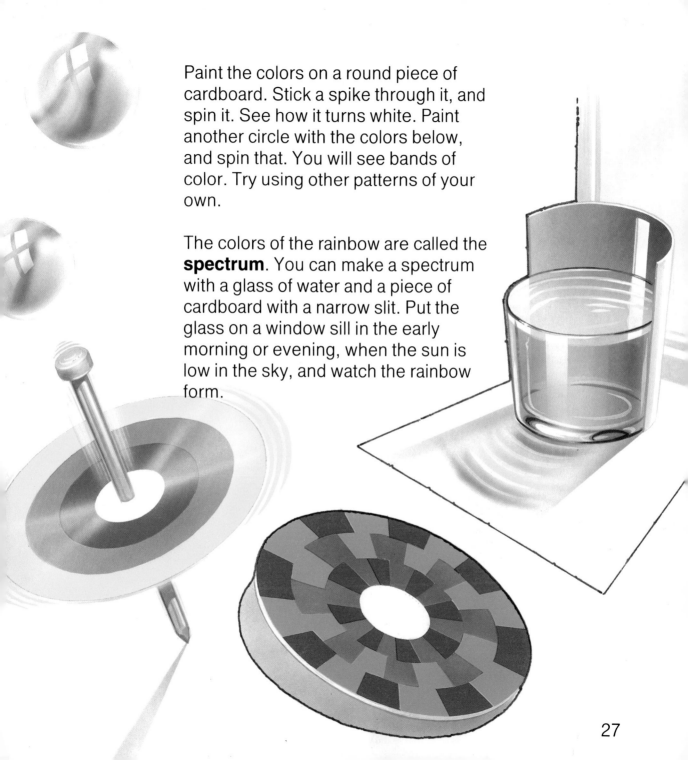

Paint the colors on a round piece of cardboard. Stick a spike through it, and spin it. See how it turns white. Paint another circle with the colors below, and spin that. You will see bands of color. Try using other patterns of your own.

The colors of the rainbow are called the **spectrum**. You can make a spectrum with a glass of water and a piece of cardboard with a narrow slit. Put the glass on a window sill in the early morning or evening, when the sun is low in the sky, and watch the rainbow form.

Color Mixing

Do you know that you can make every color there is by mixing different amounts of yellow, blue, and red paints? We call these the primary colors. Yellow and blue make green. Red and yellow make orange. See what color you make with equal amounts of red, blue, and yellow.

You can also make every color by mixing together different amounts of red, blue, and green light.

Red, blue, and green are the primary colors of light. Make different colored lights by sticking colored cellophane paper over a flashlight. Shine the beam onto a white screen, and see what colors you make. What happens when you shine red, blue, and green beams together.

The colors in television pictures are made of red, blue, and green light. Look closely at a television screen, and you will see groups of tiny colored dots.

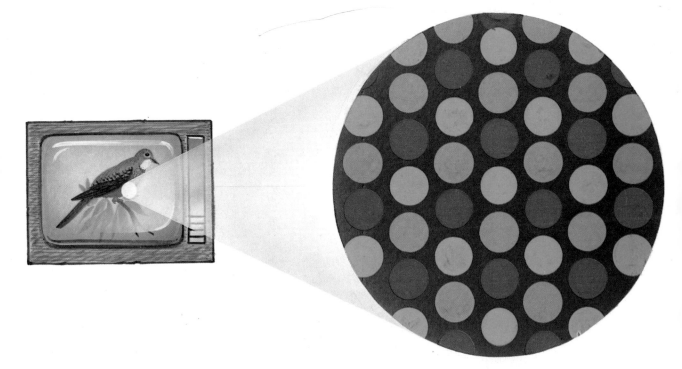

Black and White

An object looks a certain color because this is the color that it reflects. It absorbs, or takes in, all the other colors in the light. Some objects absorb all the light that falls on them. We see them as black. Others reflect all the light, and we see them as white.

Black objects also absorb the sun's heat. White objects reflect the sun's heat. Prove this yourself. Take two cans; paint one black, and the other white. Fill them with water and stand them in the sun. Use a thermometer to find which one heats up faster. When the sun goes in, see which one cools faster.

You can use the difference between black and white to make a light mill.

Make a Light Mill

1 You need a jar; strong metal foil; matte black paint; clear tape; a stick; a length of thread.

2 Cut two strips of foil about one inch by two inches. Fold them in half, and tape them together. Open them out to make a cross.

3 Tape the thread to the middle of the foil cross (spinner).

4 Paint alternate sides of the foil with black paint.

5 Tie the thread to the stick, and place the spinner in the jar. When sunlight falls on it, it should start to spin.

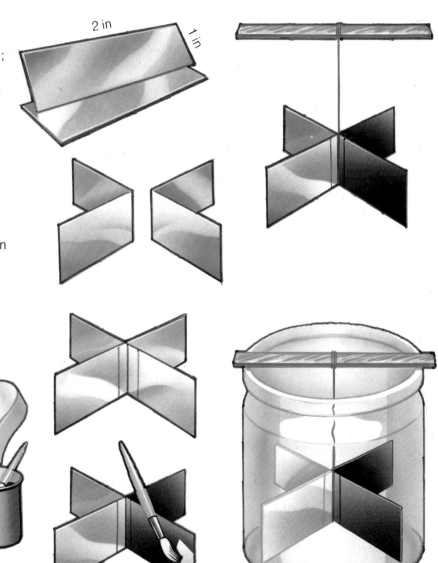

Index and Glossary